VICTORIAN BONANZA

VICTORIAN BONANZA

 Victorian Architecture of the Rocky Mountain West

TEXT BY SCOTT S. AND BETH LAMBERSON WARREN
PHOTOGRAPHS BY SCOTT S. WARREN

NORTHLAND PUBLISHING

FRONTISPIECE: *A highly detailed dragon decorates the gable of a Denver, Colorado, residence.*

FIRST EDITION
ISBN 0-87358-482-1
Library of Congress Catalog Card Number 88-43572
Manufactured in Singapore
7.5M-5/89-0201

CONTENTS

PREFACE

OPPOSITE; CLOCKWISE FROM UPPER RIGHT: *Tower detail on an 1890 Queen Anne row house in the Clements District of Denver, Colorado; A pair of window enframements on a commercial building in Leadville, Colorado; An 1888 commercial building in old Colorado City, which is now part of Colorado Springs, Colorado; Ornamental cornice on the 1885 Masonic Temple in Helena, Montana.*

For anyone who has traveled the Rocky Mountains, it would suffice to say that this is a land of imposing scale and undeniable ruggedness. Majestic peaks rake the sky, broad plains and deserts offer reprieves amidst these grand summits, and the elements reign powerful and supreme. But too, the Rocky Mountain West is a land that boasts a rich and colorful history, for despite the region's overwhelming stature, men came by the hundreds of thousands to stake out their livings and seek their fortunes. As they did, they not only settled this vast frontier, they also brought with them the trappings of civilization to which they had grown accustomed. Of these cultural amenities, the most visible, and certainly the most fascinating, are the fanciful homes and edifices that embody the Victorian spirit.

As two who have lived in the Rocky Mountain West for many years, we have long enjoyed the specific beauty that the region's Victorian buildings present. Initially, the graceful details and sculptured forms of these pretentious structures appealed to us, as did the delightful contrast between their civilized character and the dramatic backdrop of the Rockies. But, as our interest in them grew, it became apparent that here were some of the finest examples of one of civilization's greatest artistic pursuits—architectural design—in the most improbable of settings—the Rocky Mountains. We wanted to know more.

We soon discovered that relatively

little existed on Victorian architecture in the Rocky Mountains. Some books that examine Victorian building design on a nationwide scale did hint at the theme's appearance in the West, and a number of smaller publications examined the architectural manifestations in individual towns or states. But no comprehensive text that we knew of had ever been compiled. Hence, it seemed reasonable to create one ourselves.

As with most projects such as this, the magnitude of our task was not immediately apparent at the start. What looked to be a simple matter of amassing and rehashing previously published information soon grew to include much more. First, the bounds of this study, both chronological and geographical, would have to be settled. The parameters of Victorian architecture seem to expand or contract with almost every dissertation. For the sake of presenting as comprehensive a view as possible, we opted to follow a broad and somewhat simplified definition. Since the Victorian era ran from 1840 to 1900, we reasoned we would consider structures of this period that had some stylistic merit. In considering the geographic boundaries of this book, we again followed a far-reaching definition of the Rocky Mountains. Of course, the states of Idaho, Montana, Utah, Wyoming, and Colorado fell within this category, but we also

added New Mexico and Arizona, since both states present notable examples, and their development was directly related to the region as a whole. We then looked at Nevada. Here was a western state that did have some noteworthy examples of Victorian architecture, but they are found mostly in the western tier and are tied very closely to California's historical development; Nevada was subsequently dropped.

Once we had defined the scope of the book, we collected as much information as possible from state agencies and local historical organizations, various chambers of commerce, every published volume we could get our hands on, and numerous individual experts. Some information was contradictory, some was overly narrow in scope or interpretation, and some contributed little to the overall understanding of Victorian architecture in the West.

Finally, once we had armed ourselves with enough book knowledge, we took to the field. And what a big field it was. From the farthest reaches of northern Idaho and Montana to only a few miles north of the Mexican border, we crisscrossed the region, searching and then analyzing all that we found. Although the literature research we conducted was important, it was this actual in-person investigation that revealed the most useful and interesting details of this book. It also resulted in what is likely the most comprehensive index of Victorian architecture in the Rocky Mountains today.

After an introductory statement, we present a historical backdrop to illustrate the setting from which this architecture was able to develop. This is followed by a discussion on the actual architectural styles that constitute the Victorian menu of the Rockies. An inventory of specific Rocky Mountain towns and cities that still display the Victorian spirit follows, and then a look at the present and future status of Victorian architecture in the West.

One last note of interest. As we examined the topic, we discovered that academic opinions vary on occasion. For the most part, these discrepancies arose when the task of style identification was at hand. For example, what one source calls Queen Anne, another labels Victorian Eclectic. In our identifications, and in our narrative as well, we have weighed the options before presenting what we believe to be the most accurate interpretation. Certainly, some disagreement with what is presented here may arise, but then the study of any artistic medium can be nearly as subjective as the art itself.

i x

FROM LEFT: *Detail from a commercial building in Salida, Colorado; Shingle detail from the 1891 Byron Cummings House in Salt Lake City, Utah.*

Detail of the Grand Imperial Hotel built in 1883 in Silverton, Colorado; OPPOSITE: *Detail on the San Miguel County Courthouse built in 1887 in Telluride, Colorado.*

WHAT IS VICTORIAN?

When Martin Holter built his home in 1879, he no doubt wanted to erect a comfortable abode in which his family could live. Similarly, though, he was concerned not only with flaunting his status within the community, but also with current architectural tastes. As co-owner of a successful sawmill in Helena, Montana, he spared no expense in executing a masterful design. It would be a structure of modest size and yet possess an air of grandeur. Sporting fanciful half-arched windows, a mansard roof, and a striking tower centered over the main entrance, the Holter Home cast a glance toward fashionable Paris. But more importantly, it embodied the specific elegance that characterized the Victorian era of nineteenth-century America.

While the Holter House summoned the grace of France, other neighborhood homes espoused the virtues of other Old World motifs. An earlier Helena residence reflected the style of Medieval England. Others emulated Italian villas, while many commercial buildings in the city's downtown sector resembled Renaissance townhouses of urban Italy. Within the decade following 1879, lavish Queen Anne homes were gracing the streets of Helena. It was with this innate vigor that Helena, and many other western cities and towns, adopted from the past to create a new and dynamic present.

Today the homes and edifices of the Victorian era are often recognized as those structures of the 1800s that unpretentiously employed a variety of designs and embellishments to create flavorful designs. Bay windows and steeply pitched rooflines, lacy trimwork and bracketed eaves, turrets and towers, arched windows and columns: each characterized the architecture that we generally know as Victorian. But what actually is Victorian architecture? And what forces brought it about?

Quite simply, Victorian architecture is that which emanated from the Victorian era, a period denoted by the reign of England's Queen Victoria. Ascending to the throne in 1837, the monarch lived until 1901. But for simplicity's sake, the bounds of this period are often rounded off to 1840 and 1900. Despite Britain's lack of control over its former colonies, the Victorian era permeated most English-speaking countries, including the United States.

But Queen Victoria, for all her repute, had little to do with the design of buildings during her time. Rather, her sovereignty happened to parallel an era of great technological, economic, and social advance. This in turn paved the way for unprecedented experimentation in architectural aesthetics. In this country, this era of progress was especially noteworthy.

During the first days of the Victorian era, America was, for all practical purposes, an agricultural nation. At its close, however, it could boast of being a major industrial power. The inventive spirit that marked these years no doubt helped. Electric motors, sewing machines, photography, the telegraph, and telephones were but a few contrivances that arose during Victorian times. Transportation improved dramatically, as railroad lines totaling less than three thousand miles in 1840 grew to over one hundred thousand miles by century's end. The advent of farm and manufacturing machinery literally changed the way that America did business. Ushering in what is termed the Industrial Revolution, the Victorian era helped create the America we recognize today.

Changes in the nation's social facade likewise characterized the Victorian era. Education took many steps forward, as did the country's political process. Victorians developed an unquenchable thirst for knowledge, and many people were often adept at more than one vocation. Cabinetmakers might double as draftsmen, while lawyers might also be engineers. A man of Victorian times was a latter-day Renaissance man as well.

In light of this burgeoning of interests, aesthetic tastes broadened as well. Consequently, the architectural vanguard of the Victorian era was indeed one rich with variety and resplendent in tastes. But to congratulate

The 1879 Martin Holter House in Helena, Montana, recalls the splendor of Paris with its mansard roof.

turing of architectural detailings permitted their widespread use, and the upgraded scale of nineteenth-century transportation, mostly the result of expanding freight-train service, eased the distribution headaches that plagued an earlier America.

But just as a structure's exterior design was taking quantum leaps forward, so too were the conveniences of its interior. Victorian progress also saw the invention of many niceties that we take for granted today: central heating, hot and cold running water, lighting, cooking ranges, and the water closet topped the list of household improvements. Obviously, each helped to shape Victorian life in no small way.

Victorian architecture, then, is the result of both a maturing industrial landscape and the expansion of tastes that it permitted. Its buildings are the historical deposition of a period of growth that moved this country to the threshold of the twentieth century. Where the Rocky Mountain West is concerned, however, the manifestation of Victorian times also marks the region's first foray into urbanized life. While other sections of the country saw these fanciful edifices as a handy means of reflecting the deep-rooted romanticism of the day, in the Rocky Mountains they coincided with the very settlement of the land. By embracing

only the palate of the nineteenth century for its fascinating buildings would be to deliver only half of the credit due. The advances in technology that the Victorian era brought about also allowed for the wholesale dissemination of Victorian architecture. Construction methods improved dramatically as balloon framing, the use of small-dimension lumber to create a sturdy yet more versatile infrastructure, provided a practical break from the constrictions of half-timber framing. The manufac-

LEFT: *Even the carriage house of the 1884 Governor's Mansion included Victorian embellishments.*
OPPOSITE: *The Masonic Lodge, like many of Helena, Montana's, commercial buildings, resembles Renaissance townhouses of urban Italy.*

4

An early Gothic Revival home in Helena, Montana.

the Victorian venue without hesitation, the West's founding fathers purposefully bridged the gap between wilderness and civilization.

Helena's Holter Home represents the quantum leap that the West took during the second half of the nineteenth century. And, while its story is wholly fascinating, it is by no means unique. Rather, it is one that was repeated time and time again throughout the Rocky Mountains. Butte, another Montana mining town, also adopted a Victorian veneer. The tree-lined avenues of Boise, Idaho; Utah's Salt Lake City; and Cheyenne, Wyoming, were born under the venue of Victoriana. Likewise, such Colorado cities as Denver, Georgetown, Aspen, Leadville, and Durango all embraced the opulent spirit of Victorian times. Even the southwestern towns of Las Vegas, New Mexico, and Prescott, Arizona, portrayed a Victorian ambience. Ostensibly, the Rocky Mountain West can point to a Victorian past with the same pride that the East and West Coasts, the Midwest, and the South can, and this book, by examining Victorian architecture in the Rocky Mountain states, was conceived to do just that.

As a scholarly endeaver, the study of architecture can be quite perplexing to the layman. It can also, however, be of great interest when presented in a lucid and concise manner. By devoting attention not only to the styles that constitute the Victorian genre but to its historical stage in the Rocky Mountains and to the present status of these edifices as well, it is hoped that the material presented here will lift the reader to a new, more comprehensive level of understanding. To simply say that Mr. Holter's house is "Victorian" might indicate a generic interest, but to be able to identify it and understand how it arrived in the West will lead to a far better understanding of what we commonly refer to as Victorian architecture.

7

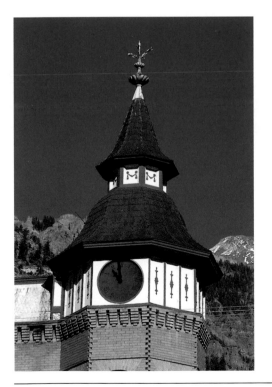

When the Victorian era began in the 1840s, the typical residence in the Rocky Mountains was a sod home, log cabin, or adobe structure. Shelter was a function of survival rather than a matter of taste. Yet, by the close of this elegant time period, some sixty years later, western towns such as Boise, Helena, Salt Lake City, Cheyenne, Denver, Albuquerque, and Prescott would sport some of the most contemporary and imaginative interpretations of the Victorian building theme. How Victorian architecture came to this land of rugged mountains and broad prairies is a story of urban conquest facilitated by a new type of settler.

Certainly architecture is the product of an imaginative mind. These people were Victorians—inventive and aesthetically inclined people. But they were also settlers. Victorians of the East were just that—Victorians. But the nineteenth-century individuals who settled the West played a dual role, for in addition to embracing the Victorian theme, they were also civilizing the mountainous frontier.

Prior to 1848 the Rocky Mountain West was an enigma. With the exception of scattered fur traders, a number of military expeditions, and a handful of religious ventures, few other vestiges of civilization existed beyond the Mississippi River. Santa Fe, a Spanish outpost established in 1609, and Salt Lake City, a Mormon enclave barely a year old (1847), offered the only notable exceptions to this rule. In 1848, however, the discovery of gold in the foothills of California's Sierras ignited the fuse of the first westward settlement explosion. This event served to shape the Rockies in two ways. First, thousands of newcomers drawn by the promise of immediate wealth traversed the Rockies on their way to the California gold fields—they were, in a sense, introduced to this vast land. Few lingered purposefully, however, as the region appeared to be little more than an enormous obstacle along the journey. The second, and most important effect, was that this mass westward migration to the gold fields set, like no other event, the precedent for the urbanization of the Rockies that followed nearly a decade later.

Before this time, the settlement of a town was a slow and deliberate process, often taking generations to progress from a rural to an urban environment. But mining, with its possibility of overnight wealth, produced what are often refered to as "boomtowns." In a matter of months or even weeks a ragged collection of tents and shanties could be transformed into a full-fledged town. While the actual mining provided the impetus for such dramatic development, it was those who followed upon the heels of these prospectors that brought about the most change. They were the components of the urbanization process,

the unfolding of an immediate community to serve the needs of mining. Because the miner devoted most of his time to his claim, support services were needed for food, shelter, and everyday necessities. Anyone with enough money could secure urban amenities previously unheard of in a newly settled area. This quick appearance of wealth created a commercial market that attracted merchants, builders, and bankers with enough business savvy to recognize the opportunities. Nearly a decade later this drama unfolded in exactly the same manner in the Rockies.

With a still-fresh vision of the California gold rush and the grand possibilities it posed, America was ready to strike at the next opportunity. The financial panic of 1857 wreaked havoc nationally, especially within the Midwest where a collapsed real estate market, poor crops, and a decline in grain prices had a devastating effect. People were ready for a second chance, which for some came with the rather inauspicious and yet widely heralded discovery of gold at the confluence of Cherry Creek and the South Platte River in 1858. Immediately, three mining camps sprang up, of which Denver was one. It was here that the urbanization of the Rocky Mountains had its start.

Within a year's time it became

evident that Denver's mineral resources were scant at best and prospectors quickly turned their attention to the mountains just west of town. In previously unheard of gulches and drainages, substantial gold finds were made, first in Gregory Gulch and then in nearby locales. By 1860 such towns as Central City, Black Hawk, and Idaho Springs were steadfastly in place. Denver, although it never earned repute as a mining community, gained prominence as a major supply center and jumping-off point for the mining districts beyond.

While the initial development of these towns was haphazard at best, it was not long before they possessed airs of permanence. If a plot of land looked suitable for a mining camp—by virtue of its proximity to a claim or its location in a level valley floor—several things took place in the progression of a town. Land could be claimed under the Homestead Act (1862) or the Townsite Act (1844) legally, while some towns were established illegally on the mining claims themselves. Town planners were often busier than the miners, selling property to the newcomers, while less official land acquisition took place when people "squatted," or simply occupied, the desirable lots.

Not all mining camps grew into towns of distinction and style; they first had to weather the early phases as an assemblage of tents and log cabins. For example, as the mineral claims produced real profits, sawmills were set up and frame buildings were constructed. Under this more permanent atmosphere, streets were put in order and municipal governments began to take shape. If a community persevered, a factor that usually hinged on the town's location as a supply hub, like Denver, or due to the magnitude of local mineral deposits, as in the case of Central City, the profile became that of an actual town. At this point, a town's commercial district was likely to progress from a row of insubstantial false fronts to a collection of two-story, well-appointed buildings. From the beginning, real estate and construction were key elements of the boom days. At first, as few miners had time to build their own houses and merchants needed commercial structures, the need was great for immediate buildings. As conditions improved, some substantial homes and edifices were in demand. Towns progressed quickly through these stages and grew into a display of fine brick buildings, as evidenced by Larimer Street, Denver's first commercial district, which in less than ten years had " . . . a remarkable grandeur and urbanity" (Brettell 1973). It was at this stage of development that Victorian architectural motifs began to take hold.

1 1

The 1891 Kitteridge Building is a grand example of Denver's early commercial buildings.

As the gold rush unfolded in the Rockies, it touched every corner of the region that might hold a promise of new-found fortune. Denver was the premier town, and newcomers to the area spread out to the west searching for new gold claims in the mountains. Within a year of Colorado's gold strikes, Idaho was beginning to experience an influx of gold seekers. Many experienced California miners found their way to these isolated locales. The Boise Basin in south-central Idaho opened up in 1862 and quickly became the most populated and productive part of the territory. As the word spread throughout the region, people who had made Colorado their initial destination often moved up to Idaho, pursuing the constant hope of a gold strike. Many of these Idaho-bound miners filtered into Montana in search of favorable routes through the rugged Bitterroot Mountains and hit upon sizable gold diggings instead. Bannack City and Virginia City were early Montana boomtowns, and Helena soon followed—a mining hub blessed with a central location that would also contribute to its well being as a supply town. The transformation was rapid: where only mountains and wilderness had reigned, men from all walks of life were coming in pursuit of their fortunes.

Even during the tragedy of the Civil War, 1861–65, the western territories continued to see an influx of people, yet the region remained isolated from the rest of the country. Travel was a considerable undertaking, as was the transportation of goods in and out of the Rockies. Urban settlements were aching for an improvement over stage-coach lines, pack trains, and freight teams. Some areas benefited from river commerce. Freight, including building material for some of Helena's first Victorian homes, was shipped up the Missouri River from St. Louis to Ft. Benton, Montana, the farthest inland river port. Lewiston, Idaho, a supply town for the Idaho gold camps, received shipments from San Francisco via the Columbia and Snake rivers. The rest of the region, however, was in a holding pattern, waiting hopefully for the railroad.

With the end of the Civil War, the country turned its attention to the exhilaration of the Transcontinental Railroad. The positive aspects of a cross-country connection were anticipated by many, especially within the anxious mining towns of the Rockies. For these towns, the railroad could raise the profitability of the mines by providing lower freight rates for shipping ore out and state-of-the-art equipment in.

The Transcontinental Railroad was completed in 1869 at Promontory, Utah, where the rails of the Union Pacific met with those of the Central Pacific.

More cross-country routes followed, and spur lines were constructed to form a rail network. For the West this marked an emergence from the stigma of an isolated frontier, and established in no uncertain terms which towns would prosper. Noted historian Duane Smith quipped that a town without a railroad had "civic bad breath."

The railroad would contribute further to the frenetic settlement process started by the gold rush, particularly in areas with few mineral resources. Wyoming, for instance, saw only a small buzz of prospecting, yet the building of the Union Pacific line brought urban expansion to her southern corridor with the towns of Cheyenne and Laramie. These towns began as construction camps, even more tenuous than mining towns. Yet they were also scenes of overt optimism, and the early residents persevered, seeing their towns through to permanent municipalities. Laramie was known as a "thirty-day town" when it was the rail camp for the Union Pacific in 1868. Yet, in the first week of the offering of town lots by the railroad, four hundred were sold, and in less than two weeks, almost five hundred buildings of one type or another had been constructed. Laramie continued to grow, supplying the railroad with rail ties and also wood

to burn in lieu of coal, which had to be shipped from the East. As the town prospered, so did the architectural attributes, many of which took Victorian aspects.

The railroad, like no other force, played a premier role with respect to Victorian architecture, especially in the Rocky Mountains. Called "the West's greatest cultural messenger in the nineteenth century" the railroad facilitated the dissemination of the country's architectural trends. The regular mail service brought the books, periodicals, and catalogs that carried the latest home styles, including plans printed in popular pattern books. The well-known *Godey's Lady's Book*, for example, published over 450 model house designs from 1846 to 1898. One had only to write to the publishers to get a full set of drawings (Wright 1980). Additionally, train travel put the architectural ideas of Chicago, New York, and even Europe within reach of the westerner. The first major American fair to premiere architectural trends and home styles was Chicago's Interstate Industrial Exposition of 1873. Manufacturers of goods for architectural use were present, displaying varieties of brick, stonework, saws, stencils, and even wood and terra-cotta detailing for interior and exterior use (Wright 1980).

Conveyed through both the exhibitions and the many publications was a national theme of beauty as the primary consideration in domestic architecture (Handlin 1979). Architecture had heavy moral influences, suggesting that a house should not only reflect the owner's current status, but what a person hoped to achieve in the not-too-distant future. The popular publication *House Plans for Everybody* admonished, "One's dwelling is an index of his character" (Handlin 1979). Within the bonanza towns of the West, these doctrines were played out with wild abandon. The residents of these infant towns were familiar with the fine architecture of Chicago and New York, as their roots were urban in nature. With a fondness for architecture that reflected the national vogue, and a zealousness for grandeur amidst the mountains, westerners brought Victorian designs to the Rocky Mountain streets.

Often a town would improve rather than expand, tearing down the first crude structures, representative of the early temporary roots, and build instead more permanent, stylized buildings. Victorian architecture was in many instances part of this second- or third-generation building effort. In some cases, a town started with Victorian architecture, particularly company towns. These were often surveyed well in advance and even had early designations for retail, industrial, and residential districts. Durango, Colorado, was planned in conjunction with the Denver and Rio Grande Railroad, whereas Anaconda, Montana, was a copper company town. Both had formal, well-executed developments, and the first buildings were often of grand style and design, preempting the shanties and log cabins of the mining camps.

Mormon settlements had a distinctive pattern of homesites as well. Based upon the design by Mormon leader Brigham Young, these predominantly agricultural communities were planned with the houses in close proximity to one another, and the crops and pasture-land located within a reasonable distance of the town. The farmers then commuted daily to their work. The streets, following a grid pattern and usually quite wide, soon had irrigation water running down either side for gardens and orchards. This establishment process served many practical purposes, including perpetuating a close-knit community and presenting a municipal setting amidst the raw terrain.

While Mormon settlement followed a more evenly paced development than the mining towns, they also took to the Victorian style for their homes and buildings. As Salt Lake City, Utah, from the East and even Europe. The copper barons and silver kings took their place in the urbanization of the region. Fading fast were the days of the pick-and-pan prospector who had discovered the mineral riches of the Rockies in the first place.

Within the cattle industry, similar growth patterns were also taking place with the formation of huge corporate enterprises. Early cattlemen had a lucrative market with the mining rush and the new towns. The railroad however, made it possible to supply the rest of the growing national population and even compete in British markets. Exploiting an ample natural resource, the free grasslands of the western territories, cattle barons began to rival the prominence of mining entrepreneurs. These events—the initial gold rush of 1859, the advance of the railroad, the silver boom, and the cattle boom—served to transform the Rocky Mountain frontier from a remote hinterland to a populated domain in the span of some forty years.

While the towns and cities of the Rocky Mountains enjoyed years of unquestionable growth, the pace could not be maintained. As the region approached the twentieth century, the character of these Victorian towns was to be permanently altered. For many, the definitive end came during 1893 when a national depression and the repeal of the Sherman Silver Purchase Act let the ax fall. The act had provided the silver economy with a false market, as the government was given a mandate to purchase the entire projected American silver production. This repeal caused many silver towns to close up shop, in turn affecting neighboring supply and industrial centers. The copper towns, however, had a good survival rate, and the gold camps enjoyed one last heyday upon the demise of the silver market. Once the economic status of the western states finally recovered, new, more contemporary building designs were in vogue. Although the Victorian era was in essence replaced, its vitality may never be surpassed in the Rocky Mountains. Today, the most prominent monuments to the industrious settlement period are the historic buildings remaining in the towns and cities founded by the wide-eyed enthusiasts of the nineteenth century.

16   18

This galvanized-metal front on the Bell Block in Silver City, New Mexico, was shipped from the St. Louis manufacturer. Such plates are common on commercial fronts throughout the Rocky Mountain West. OPPOSITE: *The galvanized-metal front of the Bell Block was made to give the appearance of carved stone.*

A STYLE FOR
EVERY TASTE

CLOCKWISE FROM UPPER
LEFT: *Gable details on*
Colorado homes:
Telluride; Durango;
Denver; Durango.

So often it seems, nineteenth-century buildings, especially those that feature fanciful facades, bay windows, or detailed trimwork, are lumped together under the catchall "Victorian." A realtor's classified ad might read, "Cute little Victorian for sale." Or an unwitting homeowner enamored with the intricacy of her abode, will boast that the charming structure is, indeed, Victorian. Such nomenclature, though, is not only incomplete, it is also, in a sense, incorrect.

Ask that realtor if the house he is selling is Gothic Revival or tell the proud homeowner that her abode is Queen Anne and confusion may set in. Technically speaking, the term "Victorian," where architecture is concerned, refers more to a time period than to one particular style. It is within this period that a variety of actual styles enjoyed some measure of popularity. Collectively, these different design movements constitute the Victorian genre, and by knowing something about each of these styles, a better appreciation of what we think of as Victorian architecture results.

The fact that stylistic classifications exist at all in architecture substantiates the premise that building design is not just a craft but an art form, for each style is a reflection of the times. Transcending both cultural and economic classes, these styles mirror a society's tastes and allude to its aspirations, perhaps like no other artistic medium. More a factor of changing preferences over time, such distinguishable variations help bring a sense of chronological

order to the continuum of architectural
evolution by breaking it up into easily
understandable components. Caution
should be exercised, however, when
considering these stylistic movements.
While a clear-cut system of classification would offer an easy and convenient
approach to understanding the history
of American architecture, it would also
be greatly oversimplified for a number
of reasons.

Architectural styles, especially
during Victorian times, fell in and out
of fashion with considerable frequency.
As we shall see, many different influences played into the rise and fall of
their popularity. The political whims
of the nation at times spurred a change
in the architectural guard. Source books
rife with sketches often inspired
builders to replicate their designs. The
advent of new construction technology
contributed to the shaping of public
tastes. Even the simple desire for something new brought about change. While
each of these stylistic movements can be
identified, their identity is often clouded
by one or more factors.

As preferences changed, the break
from one to the next was not always
clean. Rather, movements came about
over time and transition periods often
separated them. Subsequently, structures
built during such periods adopted
elements from each. As the Victorian

RIGHT: *The windows of the Elks Lodge in Ouray, Colorado, depict both Romanesque and Queen Anne influences.* OPPOSITE: *Its roofline includes the mansard roof of the Second Empire style, its arch windows are Romanesque in nature, and its fanciful brick-work is a Queen Anne detail.*

era matured, new architectural styles often repeated elements of previous styles. Such adaptation could summon the past as well as allow for more creativity, both of which were important tasks for Victorian designs. But most prevalent where the architectural language of the Rocky Mountain states during the nineteenth century is concerned was the fact that stylistic boundaries were often blurred as a result of logistics.

Since the West had no indigenous architectural style to proclaim and because most of its residents were recent transplants, design motifs were imported, usually from the East. As each eastern Victorian style ran its course of popularity, it was eventually carried to the distant Rocky Mountains via pattern books, architectural magazines, building plans, architects, or by the settlers themselves. But as these styles were disseminated through the West, a number of phenomena occurred. In some instances, a style's appearance may have been delayed as lags of up to several years often marked a movement's debut or downfall. The very fact that these designs originated elsewhere can account for such delays, especially in the earlier years of the Victorian era when communication and transportation were slow at best. Later, as communication improved, a style that took a long time to develop in

the East might suddenly appear in western communities. Similarly, some styles that were prevalent in more populated regions of the country never made more than isolated appearances in the Rockies. Most importantly, though, as these design movements appeared in the West, they often lost some of their purity. Distant as they were from fashion-conscious cosmopolitan centers of the East, westerners were not as bound by stylistic integrity but were instead free to mix and match as they

24

The stylistic influences portrayed in the Maxwell House of Georgetown, Colorado, are many. Its pedimented windows are Greek Revival in nature. Its bracket work is Italianate. The mansard roof indicates a French or Second Empire influence, and its rich use of detailing reflects the Queen Anne style.

chose. In essence, the insular towns and cities of the Rockies served as architectural melting pots. As a result, many of the Victorian homes and buildings that are found in the Rocky Mountains today exhibit not one style, but rather a combination of two or more styles. Such structures are often labeled Victorian Eclectic.

On a similar note, because of the comparatively isolated nature of western towns and cities, localized versions of Victorian-era styles often occurred. Interestingly, such departures have often led to a difference of academic opinions as to the proper labels for particular buildings and, on occasion, to the appearance of nomenclature peculiar to a single region or town. The fact that such scholarly variances do arise points out that the study of architectural history can be a subjective endeavor in itself.

For the layman this fluctuation in academic wisdom can amount to confusion when trying to understand western Victorian-era architecture, just as the blending of stylistic elements, so typical in the Rockies, can make the identification of a structure's style a formidable task. It is these very elements of unabashed humanism, though, that help make Victorian architecture of the Rocky Mountains special.

25

Greek Revival

Although Greek Revival falls within the chronological parameters set forth earlier, in terms of embracing the essence of the Victorian spirit, it did not. Its spirit, rather, was more closely related to the formality of preceding colonial themes than to the elegant lavishness of the Victorian styles. It did, however, serve as a catalyst for the birth of the Victorian spirit, and in that respect, its inclusion here is warranted.

As a recently established America sought to shed cultural influences from England, a sentiment brought to a head by the War of 1812, it adopted a new architectural form with which to construct its buildings. Prior to this concerted rejection of British roots, popular architectural styles reflected ties with the mother country, but now a change was called for. Feeling a political and spiritual bond to ancient Greece—the first true democracy—America turned to the Greek temple as a model from which to copy.

Simplistic in form yet rigid in application, the Greek temple consisted of a spartan rectangular shape topped by a broad, low-pitched roof with a triangular, or pedimented, gable. It was adorned with an entablature (that part of the structure between the pediment and the lower support) and, of course, columns. Symmetry and definitive lines added to the boldly ordered design throughout. When first applied to public edifices in the eastern United States, most of these details were faithfully replicated. Banks sported soaring colonnades of marble, while government buildings looked like something from the Acropolis. Even some Christian churches embraced this architecture of a pagan religion.

But the shortcomings of adhering to this singular architectural form soon became apparent as it was applied to more mundane structural needs such as homes. Columns were contradictory to windows (a necessity in domestic architecture) in a visual sense, not to mention expensive. Consequently, by the 1820s a more utilitarian adaptation of the Greek temple was implemented.

Keeping its box-shaped floor plan, its symmetrical facade, and its pedimented roofline, Greek Revival had its columns reduced to a more decorative feature, mostly as porch support posts or as facial and corner pilaster boards. Windows were acceptable but the arched openings of previous styles still were not. And, the all-important entablature was now simplified to a wide band of trim. In this softer, less rigid approach, Greek Revival swept a young America.

Gaining considerable popularity

Although strict interpretations of the Greek Revival style are rare in the Rocky Mountains, the 1874 Thomas Billings Home in Central City, Colorado, does feature columns, corner pilaster boards, a low pedimented roofline, and a wide band of trim.

27

during the 1830s, Greek Revival became the dominant home style in nearly every region that had been settled thus far. So accepted was it at this time that it was often called the National Style. A little more than a decade later, however, this acceptance began to wane in the eastern reaches of the country and by 1850 it had all but lost favor completely. In the deep South this fall from grace was delayed by a decade as the grand plantation mansion became the stereotypical Greek Revival abode.

More the result of timing than anything else, Greek Revival never materialized in great numbers in the Rocky Mountain region. By the time most of the West was being settled, the country's reverence to this classical theme had all but fallen in the wake of other styles. One exception, however, was Utah, where the Mormons had established a homeland during the tail end of the style's heyday. In the Salt Lake Valley, and later in other parts of the Mormon territory, Greek Revival homes appeared, usually in simplified stone versions. Elsewhere in the West, a few examples were also built but they were more isolated holdovers than the norm.

Although few in numbers in the Rockies, Greek Revival did wield some influence on other structural motifs.

Emigrants with still-fresh memories of the design, often applied Greek Revival elements to simple wood and log structures. Most common was the use of pediment-shaped decorative caps, or lintels, over windows and doorways. The inclusion of a few columns, usually around the front entrance, or as pilaster boards (a shallow projection from a wall surface designed to resemble columns), can also be attributed to Greek Revival influence.

Even after revision, Greek Revival still embraced a Utopian attitude toward form rather than a natural one. Thus, its downfall came about largely because of its unwavering attention to classical standards. What was to follow, was the beginning of the true Victorian genre.

In reacting to Greek formality, the bulk of nineteenth-century architecture in America was to follow a path that sought an even bolder statement of cavalier opulence. Certainly, Greek Revival designs would not have fit as well with the grandeur of the western landscape as did those of later styles. Its low, rectangular shape would have stood in contrast to the upward sweep of the mountains, just as its idealized symmetry would to the seeming disarray of the wilderness.

With features that were uplifting in a visual sense, and therefore in a spiritual sense as well, the Gothic Revival style was quite popular for church designs. This brick church stands in a Leadville, Colorado, neighborhood.

28

Gothic Revival

While early architectural tastes in America sought to re-create the splendor of ancient Greece, yet another period of romantic reverence for the past emerged that eventually shared in the task of replacing it. Known as Gothic Revival, design themes reminicent of Britain's Middle Ages were soon in vogue.

As nineteenth-century Americans' disdain for England faded, interest in their Anglo-Saxon roots arose. Medieval England was both a glorious era of chivalry and a hotbed of the Christian faith. Consequently, both literature and the arts adopted themes from this bygone era. For its part, American architecture borrowed some of the mainstays of the stone abbeys and castles of old England.

Quite logically, Gothic Revival had its beginnings not in this country, but in England itself. The first known example came in 1749 when a wealthy Englishman, Sir Horace Walpole, redecorated his rural retreat with Medieval detailings. Adding pointed-arch windows and even battlements to the structure, his example was soon followed by others, and for the next century, the English countryside became studded with similarly appointed edifices. It was not until the early 1800s that Gothic Revival caught on in America, and when it did, its popularity was largely due to the efforts of two men.

One of the first American examples of Gothic Revival was built in Baltimore, Maryland, in 1832 after a design by architect Alexander Jackson Davis. Davis proclaimed the virtues of Gothic architectural themes in an 1838 publication, *Rural Residences.* This book of house plans (the first of its kind in the United States) featured many Gothic examples of country homes, but with a small circulation, it did not enjoy widespread attention. His designs did, however, influence a friend of his, Andrew Jackson Downing, a landscape architect of considerable note and enthusiasm. Picking up on the Gothic style, Downing, through two subsequent pattern books *(Victorian Cottage Residences,* 1842, and *The Architecture of Country Houses,* 1850) extolled the work of Davis, thereby popularizing the style.

Gaining acceptance in the East by 1840, original Gothic Revival—using stone—was employed in only a select number of homes. When its spirit was awakened centuries later, it was again conceived in stone, requiring the skilled hands of masons. Such a faithful execution of the style was possible only for the truly wealthy. Making do, Americans instead translated the style's design themes and elements quite nicely into wood. Often called Carpenter

Gothic, this adaptation made available for a much wider audience the possibilities of the Gothic Revival theme. It was in this wooden edition that most residential examples were built.

By comparison, Gothic Revival offered considerably more freedom in design than did its classical predecessor. For the first time, floor plans could vary from the simple rectangle. They could be irregular and more complex in shape, making them better suited to satisfying living-space requirements. Such freedom in design helped pave the

The Lace House in Black Hawk, Colorado, is another fine example of the Gothic Revival style in residential architecture. Here steep-pitched-rooflines and the charactertistic pointed arch windows are combined with a lavish amount of trimwork.

30

The 1869 John Watkins House in Midway, Utah, is a classic example of the Gothic Revival style. In addition to its steep-pitched roof and its pointed-arch window, the structure also features a strong cross-wing design and some rather opulent gingerbread detailing.

way for the style's nationwide acceptance.

Similarly, its exterior appearance reflected an organic approach to design. The pointed arch, with its angular summit, was a strong Gothic Revival trademark. Mostly used in windows, the pointed arch was used repeatedly in some structures, while others featured it only once. Another identifying element, and certainly a more consistent one, was the steep gabled roof. As with the Gothic archway, such rooflines tended to draw the eye upward and would sometimes be topped with finials to add to the effect. Cross gables and dormers were often incorporated into Gothic Revival designs. Bay windows on the first floor and oriel windows (a manifestation of the bay window, usually on second-story levels) were also welcome additions, for they let more daylight into otherwise dark interiors and increased the intricacy of a design. Trimwork took on great importance. Just as stone Gothics featured a lavish amount of tracery, so too did Carpenter Gothic designs include the use of frilly and lacy woodwork, thanks to the well-timed invention of the scroll saw. On the exposed rafter ends, bargeboards of infinite designs were applied. Dripstones typically topped windows, and in the apex of gables, especially in the absence of bargeboards, aprons of various designs were placed. Collec-

tively, these detailings are known as gingerbread.

Nationally, homes in the Gothic Revival style never matched the numbers of its Greek Revival predecessor nor those of the Italianate movement that occurred at roughly the same time, a fact that was in part due to its relative complexity. In the West, the style's unadulterated acceptance followed a pattern similar to pure Gothic Revival homes, complete with pointed arches and prominent cross-gabling. Sporadically built throughout the Rockies, most of these homes date from the 1860s and are some of the earliest homes built in the area. Salt Lake City and some of its outlying communities saw several fine examples of Gothic Revival erected, a fact that was no doubt due to the area's early settlement. Helena offers early examples of the style, as do many of the first Colorado settlements such as Central City, Black Hawk, and Georgetown. More simplified versions of the Gothic theme often appeared as well. These diluted versions may have featured only certain traits, such as the steep-pitched roofline and a bay window, or the same roof with trimwork. Such manifestations are considered by many as being vernacular in design with Victorian details tacked on.

A late nineteenth-century manifestation of the Gothic theme is often

This door of a Gothic Revival church in Butte, Montana, features an added design within the archway. OPPOSITE: *The pointed-arch window is the calling card of the Gothic Revival style, especially where churches are concerned. This window is from the 1874 Presbyterian Church in Georgetown, Colorado.*

called High Victorian or Ruskinian Gothic after the architectural theorist John Ruskin. Characterized by its use of contrasting brick and stone, this reemergence was often used in the design of schools and libraries. A less-ornate version of the Gothic theme also appeared on college campuses. This substyle is appropriately called Campus Gothic.

Whereas Gothic Revival's influence in residential architecture did not rival that of other styles, it set the standard, like no other style, for nineteenth-century churches throughout the country. Once proclaimed as the only proper architecture for Christianity, Gothic Revival's historical ties to a period of religious fervor made it a likely candidate for houses of worship. Quite obviously, its tendency to uplift one's eyes also worked well in doing the same for one's spirit. Consequently, not only did churches of nearly every denomination embrace the Gothic Revival style early on but they steadfastly held on to it well into this century. The pointed arch, steep gables, and towering steeple topped with finials all contributed to the style's effect.

33

A rather simple, box-shaped Italianate house in Georgetown, Colorado. OPPOSITE: *This Italianate residence is found in Denver's Ninth Street Park Historic District, a remnant of one of the city's earliest neighborhoods.*

were often fully arched or else partially arched. They were then adorned with a decorative hood. Repeating the shape of the window, such enframements resembled an inverted U-shape and they ran the gamut of intricacy in detailing. If a simple rectangular window was used, then decorative awnings, some echoing the bracket work of the roof overhang and some pedimented, were used to liven them up. Additionally, windows were sometimes grouped in sets of two or three, and

bays were occasionally employed. Doorways typically reflected window activity.

Another Italianate feature, though its occurrence was somewhat rare, was some sort of squared tower arrangement. On more extravagant models, a full-length tower would be situated either front and center or in the crook of an L-shaped floor plan. A less overt version was the cupola, a tower rising from the center of the roof. Similarly, quoin detailing sometimes embellished

A number of Italianate commercial buildings, identified by their use of brackets on the eave, line Harrison Avenue, the main thoroughfare in Leadville, Colorado.

the structure's corners, and arcaded porches or balustrated balconies were added.

Enjoying immense popularity in many sections of the country until 1880, Italianate homes made frequent appearances in many parts of the Rockies, mostly during the 1870s and into the 1880s. Exhibiting a certain urbane look, these abodes were quite popular in such cities as Denver, Helena, Butte, Salt Lake City, and Boise, and they did make periodic appearances in many smaller towns as well. Interestingly, Italianate homes do not appear with any regularity in Colorado's high mountain towns. Although the interpretation of this fact is open to conjecture, one possibility is that the style's flat-topped roof was not suitable to handle the heavy snow loads common in this region. By comparison, most western examples are simple box-shaped affairs that left off the cupola.

Greatly outnumbering Italianate residential designs, though, were the style's nonresidential manifestations. First gracing numerous schools, banks, and railroad stations in the 1830s, the Italianate manner soon found its most common application in its adaptation to commercial fronts. Styled after the more formal Italian Renaissance townhouse, this variant of Italianate was used widely throughout. On the structure's street-side facade, Italianate windows were typically used. But most importantly, enhancement of the roof cornice with heavily emphasized bracket work was the style's trademark. In the West, where false fronts were originally built in hopes of emulating a big-city appearance, the Italianate design was a logical step forward. As a result, Italianate commercial fronts can be found in virtually every nineteenth-century town that still stands.

One method of construction that fit quite well with the Italianate commercial front was the use of prefabricated cast iron and pressed metal facades. A product of the emerging Industrial Age, whole building fronts could be manufactured in factories, shipped, and then attached to plain brick walls. These facades were designed and painted to resemble stone or wood and they were quite popular because of their durability, economy, and resistance to fire. Making their debut in New York in 1843, prefabricated facades enjoyed nationwide use well into the 1870s; in the Rockies they were common for nearly two decades beyond that. Today many examples of both conventionally constructed Italianate fronts and mass-produced versions line the streets of many mountain towns.

39

Second Empire

As American architecture continued its search for new and innovative styles, it became ever more fortified in its emphasis on both informal floor plans and striking outward appearances. Old England and rural Italy had each contributed their influence, but soon it was France's turn. From this fashionable nation of the Continent, America borrowed what is known as the Second Empire style.

Named after the reign of Napoleon III (1852–70), France's Second Empire, this stylistic movement embraced one uniquely French element: the mansard roof. Double sloped with a steep lower pitch, the mansard roof originated with the seventeenth-century architect François Mansard. The unique design was subsequently revived during Napoleon III's rule, when much of Paris, including the Louvre, was rebuilt. Two French-hosted World Expositions and prints depicting a remodeled Parisian skyline helped bring the style to this country. First appearing in America in the lates 1850s, Second Empire was a major architectural force during the 1860s and '70s nationally, and into the 1880s in the West.

The mansard roof, quite conveniently, added considerable head-room to attics, turning them into usable living

ABOVE: *A Second Empire residence in Lake City, Colorado.* OPPOSITE: *This 1879 Helena, Montana, home, with its mansard roof, is a fine example of the Second Empire style.*

spaces. Consequently, no Second Empire house was less than two stories high. Since light was a necessity in these top floors, dormer windows, almost without exception, broke up the roofline. The shape of the roof's lower pitch could be straight-edged, concave, convex, or S-shaped, and molding was typically used to bind both edges of the lower roof slope.

Below its characteristic roof, many of Second Empire's detailings were borrowed from the Italianate style. The windows were usually embellished in the Italianate manner, and the roof's overhang, while not as exaggerated, often featured brackets. On occasion, the same square towers that graced Italianate designs also adorned Second Empire homes.

While Second Empire's freehanded adaptation of design elements from other styles might raise questions about its purity, such mixing of stylistic vocabularies was common during the second half of the century. Additionally, the mansard roof was so distinctive that it was nearly a style unto itself. Even when placed on buildings lacking any specific detailing, the resulting structure could still be considered Second Empire. With its classification hinging on this one distinctive element, Second Empire is perhaps the easiest of all Victorian styles to identify.

Within the Rockies, as well as in the Midwest and the East, Second Empire homes were quite popular and many fine examples of the style can still be found in most western towns and cities today. Certainly, much of Second Empire's popularity can be attributed to the very fact that it came from Paris. This French city was considered an important center of art and fashion by nineteenth-century Americans, and despite the fact that the mansard roof was already two hundred years old, it was still thought of as being very contemporary.

Because of this perceived grandeur, Second Empire's influence was also strong in areas other than residential use. In addition to gracing schools, government buildings, and even factories, the French theme was particularly suited to hotel architecture. By topping a structure with a mansard roof, it was hoped that the splendor of Paris could be re-created for the guests. In the "uncivilized" Rocky Mountains, such attention to elegance was very important. Consequently, the pride and joy of many western towns was a grand hotel in the French tradition.

Completed in 1897, the Hotel Metlen in Dillon, Montana, illustrates the popularity of the mansard roof on hotels of the day. The desired effect was to create a building of grandeur and elegance.

42

Romanesque Revival

OPPOSITE: *The 1893 Sewall House in Prescott, Arizona, with its assymetrical massing, typifies the Queen Anne style.*

BELOW RIGHT: *This building in Durango, Colorado is representative of the Romanesque Revival's adaptation to commercial structures. It features both prominent arches and rough-cut stone masonry.*

Developing during the same time period as Queen Anne, but exuding a far different ambience, was Romanesque Revival. As its name suggests, it looked to classical Rome for some of its inspiration. This style, however, was also closely tied to one particular architect.

Although most prevalent from 1880 to 1900, Romanesque designs were experimented with during the 1840s and '50s by various architects. Nothing of note came of the motif, however, until Boston architect Henry Hobson Richardson (1838–86) took up the style. Richardson had designed many structures in Second Empire and Queen Anne but in the 1870s he began work in this newer vein. Most influential of Richardson's work is the Trinity Church in Boston. Designed in 1872, this structure won an important architectural competition and subsequently helped establish, like no other building, the theme's popularity. Appropriately, this style is often called Richardsonian

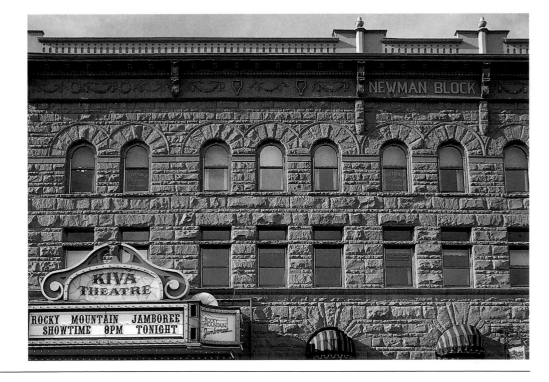

This Durango, Colorado, home, with its broad arches and rough-cut masonry construction, is Romanesque Revival in design. Because of its rather cumbersome elements, Romanesque homes never rivaled other styles in numbers.

Romanesque.

Undoubtedly, the most dutiful of Romanesque Revival's elements was its round, broad arch. Previous styles such as Italianate had incorporated rounded arches in their designs but none emphasized this Roman invention like Romanesque did. Applied to window and door openings, and occasionally to porch supports, this key element is wholly recognizable.

A second characteristic that was nearly as important as the archway was the use of rough-faced stone masonry as a building material. Usually employing large, rectangularly cut stone, Romanesque Revival structures had a very weighty look about them. Reinforcing this look were the style's typically deep-set windows and doorways. Other elements that were not as consistent included towers (usually round with a conical-shaped roof), corbels, short columns of a decorative nature, and chevron- and diamond-shaped design patterns.

The Dolores County Courthouse in Rico, Colorado, is a fine example of the use of the Romanesque design in brick.

Because of the style's very nature, Romanesque Revival buildings were expensive to construct; consequently, few houses were built in this style. Requiring a large design to apply its bulky elements properly, those homes that did embrace the Romanesque venue are usually considered to be mansions. In most of the West's smaller towns, such designs are absent, but some cities are graced by their extraordinary opulence. Two notable locales are Pueblo and Denver, both along Colorado's Front Range.

While the style precluded frequent appearances in residential form, it did wield considerable influence where public edifices were concerned. Beginning with Richardson's Trinity Church, Romanesque Revival was a favored style for many institutional and commercial applications. Besides churches, its stout and powerful appearance could not only reflect a building's use but enhance the public's perception of it as well. Banks, for example, could impart a sense of stability and confidence, while government structures could exude a look of stateliness with Romanesque Revival designs. Most towns of the Rockies, as well as of other regions, still have such muscular edifices in use, and their effect is no less impressive today.

51

A VICTORIAN BONANZA

CLOCKWISE FROM BOTTOM LEFT: *Roof details on commercial buildings in Leadville, Colorado; and,* BOTTOM RIGHT, *in Ouray, Colorado.*

The Rocky Mountain states are rich with the fanciful and opulent edifices of the Victorian era. But the national focus on Victorian architecture highlights the East and West Coasts, or the Midwest, with only a brief scan across the mountainous states. This oversight, until recently, could be attributed to the region's own lack of publicity of its historical treasures. The Rocky Mountain's cultural resources have begun to attract an enthusiastic visitor, one who takes great pleasure in piecing together the past by using the clues of the present. Tourism bureaus and chambers of commerce are now marketing the Victorian elements of their state or community by putting together walking or driving tours and enlisting the help of private historical groups as well.

The National Register of Historic Places will hint at the scope of a town's history and these listings are usually available for a small fee from the state historical offices. While helpful in researching this book, they failed to identify the town's historical character. This chapter, therefore, is dedicated to the presentation of the Rocky Mountain towns and cities that embody Victorian architecture.

Ostensibly, nearly every town and city that has its roots in the nineteenth century has at least one standing example of Victorian architecture within its bounds. But the purpose here is not to include every last manifestation of the theme in the West, but rather to present a listing of those places that offer a more comprehensive overview of the Victorian manner.

As each town beckons with its fine homes and commercial districts, dig a little deeper to unearth the elements that brought each municipality to life. When traveling from one town to the next, keep a sharp eye out for lesser-known examples and make your own discoveries.

Here then is a selected guide to some of the best examples of Rocky Mountain Victorian architecture. It is hoped that this will not only instill a broader understanding of our western heritage but perpetuate a desire to safeguard it as well.

The 1894 Heritage House in Kanab, Utah, was stumbled upon quite unexpectedly by the authors. Such little-known "discoveries" abound throughout the West in countless small, out-of-the-way towns.

Colorado

Of all the Rocky Mountain states, Colorado saw the greatest amount of both gold- and silver-mining activity. From the start of the region's rich era of mineral exploration, Colorado was at the forefront with the first gold strikes in what is now Denver. Dozens of profitable finds quickly followed, and by the end of the century, nearly every corner of the state's mountainous western half had experienced one sort of boom or another.

Resulting from this euphoria of mining activity was an opulent and widely varied way of life for nineteenth-century Coloradoans. Hundreds of towns sprang up at the foot of the mountains, in the high alpine valleys, along steep mountainsides, and even above timberline. Although many of these mining towns did not survive the various economic downturns that hit the state, the strongest and best of them did. As a result, a number of Colorado towns and cities today offer spectacular visions of the region's Victorian past. From such large metropolises as Denver and Colorado Springs to small mountain towns like Ouray and Silverton, Colorado's collection of Victorian homes and structures is unrivaled in both number and diversity among western states.

Denver's 1890 Tivoli Brewery, with its Second Empire tower, has recently undergone renovation and is now a fashionable shopping mall.

DENVER

What started as the first mining camp in the region, eventually grew to become one of the largest metropolitan areas in the Rocky Mountain states. Denver, with its beginning dating to 1858, was established at the confluence of Cherry Creek and the South Platte River by the first prospectors to hit the Rockies. Although not much gold was found, the Queen City of the Plains was destined to become a city of considerable importance.

The first structures built in Denver were simple log cabins of vernacular design. But the architectural face of the city soon began to take shape as Victorian embellishments were added to these houses. These, in turn, were followed by the manifestation of true Victorian designs. A widespread fire, which destroyed much of the city, was the impetus for an 1863 town ordinance that required the use of brick and other fireproof materials. Consequently, very few wood structures are still standing in Denver.

Denver's architectural development has been compared to that of Chicago's, for that is where much of its aesthetic stimulus originated. Many buildings of both cities were designed by professional architects, and each town had architectural magazines in circulation.

Constructed in 1884, the Italianate Clements row houses of the Clements Historic District in Denver, Colorado, are reminiscent of San Francisco's bayfronts.

Denver's most prolific construction period began in 1879 and ran until the silver crash of 1893. During this time, thousands of fine homes and many grand commercial buildings were erected.

Despite the fact that urban renewal was rampant in Denver during the 1960s, there are still many Victorian structures standing. As a city of nearly half-a-million residents, Denver has hundreds of historic sites and districts. One such district is the Clements District, a small but richly varied neighborhood a few blocks north of city center at Tremont Place and 21st Street. Platted in 1864, most of the district's homes date from the 1870s and '80s and offer some exquisite models of both Italianate and Queen Anne styles.

Another restored neighborhood that dates from the same time period is the Ninth Street Historic Park in the heart of the Auraria Community College campus. Once part of a much larger neighborhood, the district's dozen or so standing structures are all that survived one of the Denver Urban Renewal Authority's (DURA) most ambitious projects. Although these remaining buildings were also slated for demolition, Historic Denver, Inc.,

stepped in and managed to convince DURA to leave them. Today, these mostly Second Empire and Italianate abodes serve as much-coveted office space for the campus administration.

Other Victorian residential areas abound in Denver, some of which can be found in the vicinities of the Molly Brown Mansion and Cheesman Park. Here, many mansions were constructed around the turn of the century, reflecting the wealth that Denver enjoyed in its early years.

Although many of the city's commercial buildings were razed, a few examples still remain. Dotting Denver's glass-and-steel-tower-studded skyline are some nineteenth-century stone edifices, most reflecting detailings of the Romanesque Revival style. A well-known center of early commercial structures is Larimer Square. Noted as the place where Denver had its start, this one-block area went through an early day version of urban renewal as the commercial structures that we see today replaced the original buildings of the city's late-nineteenth-century building boom. Today Larimer Square is one of Denver's most fashionable restaurant and shopping areas.

CENTRAL CITY/BLACK HAWK

The streets of Central City, Colorado, are tightly packed with a collage of Italianate commercial fronts. It is a colorful sight that is reminiscent of the town's early days.

The first gold strike of any real size in the Rockies came on 6 May 1859, thirty miles west of Denver in Gregory Gulch. Named after the discoverer, John Gregory, this field produced over ten million ounces of gold, and within a month of the intial strike, the area's population grew to fifteen thousand. By year's end a town, Central City, was in place.

As Colorado's first boomtown, Central City rivaled Denver in size for years, and it was once considered as a possible site for the capitol. It was a bustling city intent on flaunting its wealth and cultured ways: in 1861 a stage group delivered its first performance, an opera house was soon built, fine hotels were completed, and many Victorian homes were constructed. In 1874 a fire destroyed much of the original downtown sector, but brick, stone, and cast-metal-facade commercial structures were soon built to replace the lost buildings.

Today, Central City is a lively town with colorful storefronts lining its narrow, steep-pitched streets. Tightly packed together, these Italianate commercial fronts go a long way toward recalling the town's early days. On the hillside just north of Central City's main thoroughfare is a splendid selection of Victorian homes: Greek Revival, Gothic Revival, Italianate, and Second Empire are the predominant stylistic themes. Some interesting homes can be found on the south side of the gulch as well.

About a mile east of Central City is the town of Black Hawk. Known more for its smelter than its mineral deposits, the founding of Black Hawk likewise came during the late 1850s. Although the narrow canyon in which Black Hawk is situated prevented the town from rivaling Central City in size, it did match its neighbor in unbridled growth for a time. Among its accomplishments were the region's first narrow-gauge railroad, the Colorado Central that came up from Denver, and the first cemetery. Architecturally, Black Hawk's collection of nineteenth-century buildings does not compare with those of Central City, but it is the site of some fine examples just the same. Among them is the aptly named Lace House, a wonderful Gothic Revival design greatly embellished with intricate trimwork.

65

IDAHO SPRINGS

Another Colorado town that had its beginnings with an 1859 gold strike is Idaho Springs, also west of Denver. On a cold January day, George Andrew Jackson panned a bit of gold from a frozen sandbar in Chicago Gulch with a cup. Returning in April with supplies and twenty-two men, he staked out a claim. Soon a town was established that went under a variety of names. *Idahoe*, an Arapahoe word meaning "Gem of the Mountains" was eventually chosen. "Springs" was added as a reference to a nearby hot spring.

Along Idaho Springs's main residential streets (Virginia Street and Colorado Boulevard) are a variety of fine homes dating from the late 1800s. The predominant style is Queen Anne, although a few Italianate houses were also built. Intermixed with these are several houses from the early part of this century, reflecting some post-Victorian styles. Along Miner Street is the town's commercial sector with its few blocks of colorful Italianate fronts. A walking tour brochure was printed in 1987 that depicts many of these homes in photos, then and now.

66

This Queen Anne is one of many Victorian homes that grace Colorado Boulevard in Idaho Springs, Colorado.

GEORGETOWN / SILVER PLUME

Built in 1867, the Hamill House in Georgetown, Colorado, typifies the Gothic Revival style. Note the solarium, which dates to the early 1880s. It is owned by the Georgetown Historical Society.

One of the finest collections of Victorian homes in the Colorado Rockies can be found in Georgetown, almost an hour west of Denver. Here, in the bottom of Clear Creek Canyon, rich gold and then silver lodes resulted in the establishment of a classic manifestation of Victorian tastes.

Missing out on the Central City bonanza by only a few weeks, George and David Griffith instead followed Clear Creek farther upstream where, in June of 1859, they found a promising amount of gold. Immediately establishing the Griffith Mining District, George assumed the task of district recorder, and the developing town was subsequently named after him. Greatly outdistancing the amount of gold discovered in and around Georgetown were its large silver deposits. Once silver became a coveted commodity, Georgetown and Silver Plume, a few miles up-canyon, enjoyed the benefits of the silver boom. It is said that during the 1880s, Georgetown was Colorado's third largest city and that it was the world's leading producer of silver.

In 1893 the dramatic devaluation of silver dealt a powerful blow to Georgetown and Silver Plume, and in the decades that followed, the towns were neglected. As Colorado's Front Range began to blossom in the 1950s, however, these nearby mountain towns were once again noticed, not for their mineral stocks but for their historic wealth. In 1966 the Georgetown–Silver Plume National Historic Landmark District was designated to encompass both towns, the Georgetown Loop Railroad, and much of the surrounding mountainsides.

The fact that Georgetown served as the home of mine owners, successful merchants, doctors, and others of

67

wealth, while Silver Plume was more of a working-class town, is reflected quite strongly in their architecture. Silver Plume is today a collection of simple falsefronts and small houses, many of which display only tacked-on Victorian details. Georgetown, on the other hand, is characterized by its collection of truly Victorian abodes, presenting a generous cross-section of styles, where little was spared in construction. Two architectural highlights are the Hamill House, an 1867 Gothic Revival design that was expanded considerably beginning in 1874, and the Maxwell House. Constructed on a hill by a lucky grocery store owner in 1890, the Maxwell House embodies an eclectic combination of Queen Anne, Greek Revival, Second Empire, and Italianate, and was once cited as one of the top ten Victorian homes in the country. A booklet entitled *Guide to the Georgetown–Silver Plume Historic District* provides an in-depth look at these two buildings, as well as dozens more in the Georgetown area.

BOULDER

Originally settled soon after Denver, Boulder began as a mining town, but soon became more prominent as a supply base for prospectors heading into the mountains beyond. Its residents were quick to learn the benefits of supplying the miners with equipment, food, housing, and even entertainment. Because of its reliance on this comparatively more stable economy, Boulder's growth was more deliberate than that of most mining centers.

As early as 1860, Boulder was at the forefront of education in the region, for it was during that year that the first school in Colorado was built. It was also then that some of the town's citizenry began lobbying to bring a university there. In 1874 they captured that designation and two years later the University of Colorado's Main Building was completed. Today, Old Main still holds court over the university campus and it, along with a number of other nineteenth-century and early twentieth-century buildings, constitutes the Norlin Quadrangle National Historic District.

Complementing Boulder's educational heritage is its collection of historic homes and mansions. Many of these can be found in one of the town's earliest neighborhoods, the Mapleton Hill area. Here, along shady avenues, several Victorian (Italianate, late-Gothic, and Queen Anne) and post-Victorian residences are found.

Embracing the heart of Boulder's business district is the Pearl Street Historic Commercial District. With four blocks of Italianate storefronts to

LONGMONT

A dozen miles northeast of Boulder, and equidistant from the foothills of the Rockies, is the quiet community of Longmont. Settled in 1871 by a group of transplanted Chicagoans, this city never harbored illusions about striking it rich with gold or silver, being so far from the mountains. Rather, it eventually grew into an agricultural center by taking advantage of the fertile St. Vrain River drainage. Absent here were the seedier entrapments of most mining towns. Hard work and morality were instead the important items.

Just as important, though, were the cultural niceties to which these mid-westerners had grown accustomed. Architecturally, this resulted in the building of many Victorian and early twentieth-century homes in Longmont's residential sectors. Today, each of its two principal neighborhoods is a historic district. The East Side Historic District contains many of the original abodes built during the first years of the town. These include several examples of the Italianate and Queen Anne styles. The West Side Historic District includes homes built, for the most part, shortly after the turn of the century and is therefore more post-Victorian in design.

The Arnett House in Boulder, Colorado, represents many late nineteenth-century manifestations of the Gothic Revival design.

work with, Boulderites have turned what could have been an area of urban blight into a lively and colorful mall for pedestrians. The Pearl Street District is a shining example of how economically successful a rehabilitation project can be.

69

FORT COLLINS

Originally established as a military camp in 1862, Fort Collins was not officially incorporated until 1873. A small village of farmers, the town's first years were tenuous at best. It was in 1879, however, that things turned around, for that was when the Colorado Agricultural College, now Colorado State University, opened. With the school in place, more stable economic times ensued.

Today Fort Collins's architectural highlights include a scattering of Victorian homes throughout the city. Of particular note is the Avery House, a fine stone mansion dating from 1879. The Poudre Landmarks Foundation operates tours of the building and is currently restoring it throughout. Another vestige of Victoriana in Fort Collins is Old Town. A national historic district, this sector includes many of the city's original commercial buildings. With some streets closed to traffic, and a variety of shops and restaurants, Old Town is somewhat reminiscent of Boulder's Pearl Street Mall.

COLORADO SPRINGS/ MANITOU SPRINGS

Somewhat of a paradox, the founding of Colorado Springs stemmed not from mining but instead from the state's current dominant industry, that of tourism. In 1870 General William Palmer, a prominent figure in Colorado's history, organized the Denver & Rio Grande Railroad with hopes of connecting Denver with El Paso and Mexican railways beyond. Palmer's line, which eventually did span the southern tier of Colorado, reached the vicinity of Pikes Peak in the autumn of 1871. There, adjacent to a small mining-supply town known as Colorado City, he established a new town, Colorado Springs. Because of the location's beauty, Palmer envisioned his city to be a fashionable resort among the splendor of the Rocky Mountains. Indeed his plan worked, and the Springs served as a retreat for wealthy easterners for many years.

Architecturally, the Colorado Springs area offers a diverse collection of styles. Running north from the downtown area are the large and stately residences that line Wood, Cascade, and Tejon avenues. In addition to the many renditions of the Queen Anne motif, several Victorian Eclectic homes that cross Queen Anne with Shingle and Colonial Revival themes are present. The Old Colorado City Historic District features a number of fine commercial buildings, an element that seems conspicuously absent from downtown Colorado Springs. Manitou Springs, a resort town founded in 1872 around a mineral spring, not only presents several splendid examples of conventional Victorian styles, it is also home to a number of Shingle-style homes.

PUEBLO

First established in 1859, the city of Pueblo marks the site of a stockade built in 1806 by the explorer Zebulon Pike on the shore of the Arkansas River. At that time, lands north of the river belonged to the United States under the Louisiana Purchase, while those to the south were still under the jurisdiction of the Spanish. When the gold strikes of the late 1850s drew thousands to Colorado, Pueblo marked the establishment of an early Anglo settlement.

Owing its growth first to the gold in the nearby mountains, Pueblo soon grew into a major transportation center as Palmer's railroad entered the town in 1872. By 1890 four different railroads reached Pueblo. During this time, several smelters were constructed, making the town a major smelting capital for the Rockies. At the turn of the century the C.F.&I. steel mill was established, further bolstering Pueblo's industrial base.

Thanks to its strong economic foundation, Pueblo saw many fine public edifices and homes constructed during the Victorian era. Embracing Pueblo's commercial area is the Union Avenue

Historic District. Included are several blocks of storefronts dating mostly from the 1880s and '90s. Of particular note is the Union Depot, a large stone station built in 1889. Among the city's residential areas, several fine Queen Anne, Romanesque Revival, and other lesser styles are found along the avenues on the far side of the Arkansas River. At the center of this neighborhood is the Pitkin Place Historic District, home to many fine stone mansions. Other notable sites in the vicinity are the 1890 Governor's Mansion and the 1891 Rosemont House, both of which feature the rough-cut masonry work of the Romanesque tradition.

CANON CITY

Thanks to its mild climate, plentiful irrigation water, and fertile soil, Canon City has long been an important supply town for mining activity in the Colorado Rockies. From its beginnings around 1860, the town has counted crop and livestock production as two of its economic mainstays. In 1870 a territorial prison was erected (even then such a facility meant economic stability) and the Denver & Rio Grande Railroad reached the community by 1874. Because of these factors, Canon City offers a rich and somewhat surprising collection of Victoriana.

Certainly the most visible pieces

one of the town's side streets. Several other churches from the nineteenth century are likewise still in use, and a small number of mostly Second Empire and Queen Anne homes mark the town. Many of the town's edifices have received good upkeep over the years, since it is a popular summertime retreat.

OURAY

Nestled in a deep mountain canyon a dozen or so miles north of Silverton is the picturesque town of Ouray. First settled in 1875 by prospectors who had wandered over from Silverton, the town was established the following year when a promising lode was discovered. Over the years Ouray has managed to ride out the cyclical depressions that often hurt other mining towns. During the silver crash of 1893 it was able to get by on its gold production. In 1896 the opening of the nearby Camp Bird Mine meant several more years of prosperity, and during this century it has managed to develop a healthy tourism economy thanks to its sizable geothermal resources.

Because of its long-standing prosperity, Ouray's architectural treats are many and have been, for the most part, meticulously cared for. Many of its homes present textbook examples of the Queen Anne style. The Ouray County Courthouse, a block from Main Street,

is a superb piece of civic architecture. Of the town's commercial buildings, the 1888 Wright's Opera House wonderfully illustrates the use of pressed-metal facades. The Elks Lodge, across the street from the Opera House, is something of a latter-day Victorian montage. Constructed in 1904, this beautiful, red brick building includes Second Empire, Romanesque, and Queen Anne elements all in one structure. An exception to the town's loving embrace of its Victorian past is the Beaumont Hotel built in

The Kullerstrand Home (an 1895 Queen Anne design) in Ouray, Colorado, is representative of the town's rich architectural heritage. OPPOSITE: *This Telluride, Colorado, home, like many of the town's Victorian residences, has been lovingly restored.*

7 8

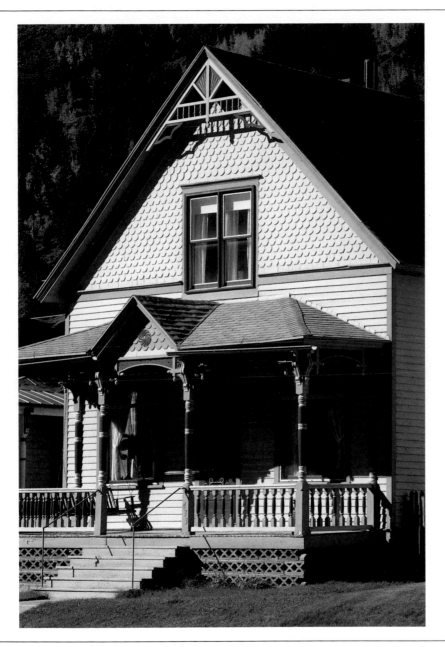

1886. A grand French-influenced monstrosity, this hotel was once the pride of the town, but for years has sat boarded up and useless. A guide to a walking tour of Ouray is available from the Chamber of Commerce.

TELLURIDE

Like Aspen and Crested Butte, Telluride is today a world-renowned ski resort, but it sprouted from the same roots as did other San Juan Mountain towns of the 1870s. Originally known as Columbia, Telluride was once one of several camps along the San Miguel River. Located closer to the best mines in the area, though, the town soon surpassed the others. Although the name is likely a reference to a gold-bearing ore called tellurium found in the area, some say it was derived from the phrase, "To hell you ride," a reference to the city's wild early days. During the 1880s Telluride progressed slowly, mostly as a result of its isolation. In 1890 Otto Mears brought his narrow-gauge railroad to the town, and a boom of several years ensued.

Thanks to its current life as a ski town, Telluride's many Victorian homes now share the avenues with several opulent neo-Victorians. At times it is difficult to discern the old from the new. A printed walking tour is available, though, and it helps in

*The Third Avenue
Historic District in
Durango, Colorado, is a
broad, tree-lined street
with many grand
Victorian and post-
Victorian residences.*

identifying Telluride's original structures. Most of Telluride's finer Queen Anne homes are found along Columbia and Galena avenues on the hillside above Colorado Avenue, the town's main thoroughfare. A block south of Colorado Avenue, along Pacific Avenue, is what has long been called Finn Town. As a community of both Finnish and Swedish laborers, a collection of rather simple boarding houses and other tenements stands that once housed these immigrants.

DURANGO

Durango originally stood as two towns. First there was Animas City, another town that came about with the signing of the Brunot Treaty in 1873. Like other mining communities of the San Juan Mountains, Animas City rose within weeks of the fateful transfer of land. Prospering for several years, the town anticipated even greater growth when the Denver & Rio Grande Railroad came to the area in 1880. But the tracks stopped two miles south, and there a new city, Durango, was founded and soon outgrew the original

community. By 1882 the first smelter was built in Durango, making it an important shipping point for ore. Combining its mining economy with healthy ranching and tourist industries, Durango has stood as the major center of southwestern Colorado ever since.

Although scattered throughout the city, the strongest concentrations of Victorian architecture are today found in and around the downtown sector. There, two national historic districts encompass spectacular collections of both residential and commercial architecture. The Third Avenue District offers several tree-lined blocks of rather lavish examples of the Queen Anne, Neoclassical, and Colonial Revival styles. Along the avenues east of Third are scattered many more, less grandiose Victorian homes. The downtown commercial district includes many well-preserved Italianate commercial fronts and is today a bustling shopping area. One other concentration of Victorian homes is found across the Animas River along West Second and Third avenues, between 16th and 25th streets.

81

New Mexico

Of all the Rocky Mountain states, New Mexico boasts the lengthiest historical chronology. Santa Fe was established by the Spanish in 1609. For more than two centuries New Mexico existed virtually isolated from the rest of the continent. And, while some of the earliest mining took place during the seventeenth and eighteenth centuries, it was not until the coming of the railroad in the 1870s and '80s that the Victorian manner gained a substantial footing in the state.

Today, when most people think of New Mexican architecture, images of earthtone pueblolike adobe structures come to mind. Indeed, much of the state's buildings are low-profile, stuccoed affairs, but there are a few strongholds of Victorian design within this south-western domain. Generally speaking, the appearance of Victorian architecture can be traced to communities that felt a strong Anglo presence during the late-nineteenth century. All but one of the cities discussed saw such influence brought in as a direct result of the railroad, while the last came about through mining interests. Although these towns are isolated examples of the Victorian theme, they offer rich and wholly fascinating collections just the same.

SANTA FE

As a long-time Spanish outpost, Santa Fe is primarily a town of adobe. There are, however, a handful of fine Victorian structures scattered throughout the city. Some of these are found along East Palace Avenue, while most of the others stand in the vicinity of the train station. Interestingly, most of these buildings have blended such Victorian components as brackets, bay windows, and mansard roofs with the earthen look of adobe-type plastering. Discovering these small but beautiful Victorian details in the midst of this Hispanic-flavored city is a special treat for connoisseurs of Victorian architecture.

ALBUQUERQUE

Another somewhat surprising find of Victorian architecture comes in Albuquerque, the state's largest city. As with Santa Fe, much of Albuquerque's celebrated architecture is distinctly southwestern in nature, but a few blocks east of the city center is a neighborhood called the Huning Highlands. Platted in 1880 by Franz Huning and John Phelan, this area is considered Albuquerque's first suburb.

Today, Albuquerque's Huning Highlands is much as it was at the turn of the century. Few additions have been made and most of its original architecture still stands. The area has suffered some deterioration, due to years of neglect, but a visit will reveal a fine collection of Victorian homes just the same. Most prominent of the styles represented here are Italianate and Queen Anne.

LAS VEGAS

Originally established in 1835 by Hispanic settlers from the Rio Grande Valley, Las Vegas did not see Victorian architecture until 1879 when the railroad arrived, bringing with it not only a new architectural face but a cultural one as well. Received with mixed emotion, the railroad passed a mile east of the original town's plaza, and it was there that East Las Vegas was established to service the line.

Victorian buildings sprang up in both municipalities—separate until 1970—and today many fine structures still stand. Around old Las Vegas's Plaza are several Italianate commercial structures, including the large 1881 Plaza Hotel. East of the now-defunct boundary are two residential areas, each centered around a city park. The Carnegie Park Historic District (named after the Carnegie Library constructed there in 1903) features a superb mix of Italianate, Second Empire, Queen Anne, and post-Victorian homes, and surrounding Lincoln Park, several blocks to the

Arizona

Arizona never enjoyed the elegant invasion of Victorian building designs to the same degree as other western states. And certainly, the strong influence that more traditional southwestern architectural themes wielded in this desert empire is partly to blame. As with New Mexico, an affinity for Spanish and Pueblo designs determined much of what was built. In addition, missions reminiscent of California's Spanish Colonial days also made occasional appearances in Arizona. (Tucson has good examples of this.)

But Arizona, thanks to its rugged terrain and the ferocity of its Indian population, remained comparatively isolated from the rest of Anglo America for some years. With only rare exceptions, the territory did not witness a mineral boom until very near the turn of the century when large copper deposits were finally exploited. At that time, such towns as Jerome, Bisbee, Globe, and Miami effectively came into being. One very notable exception to Arizona's come-lately status with respect to mining and Victorian architecture is the town of Prescott.

Near the end of the nineteenth century, no corner of the West lay untouched, and even Arizona was feeling the effects of an expanding civilization. The railroad, arriving in the state during the 1880s, made the establishment of towns feasible, and it was then that the predominantly agricultural community of Phoenix came into its own. Phoenicians graced their city with many Victorian homes and edifices, but today, only a few remain. Scattered about the Phoenix metropolitan area, some of these Queen Anne homes rival any in the nation in splendor and detailing and it is sad to think of what was lost under the guise of progress.

Some of Arizona's other cities contain examples of the Victorian architectural theme as well, but like Phoenix, most are only isolated manifestations rather than complete collections. Flagstaff, for example, does contain a few fine commercial edifices from the late nineteenth century but not enough to justify a full discussion. Two Arizona locales that do warrant inclusion are Prescott and Bisbee.

These are two of many Victorian homes that stand along Prescott's architecturally rich Mount Vernon Avenue. Both have been lovingly cared for over the years.

PRESCOTT

In 1863, the year that Arizona became a United States territory, gold was discovered near the site that was to become the town of Prescott. Founded one year later, Prescott was established as the territorial capital, and from its start was intended to be a well-ordered town. With a grid pattern of streets and a courthouse block dominating the center of town, it resembled many eastern and midwestern towns of the day. Although the capital designation was lost for good in 1889 to Phoenix, a strong economic base developed on the region's rich mining, agricultural, and timber resources. Marked by accelerated growth, the last two decades of the nineteenth century saw much of Prescott's architectural growth.

Today, many of Prescott's streets are tree-lined and graced by stately Queen Anne mansions. Of these, the most impressive collection of Victorian houses is found along Mount Vernon Avenue, a few blocks east of the city center. For most of its length, colorful

88

The Marks House, built in 1894 on Nob Hill in Prescott, Arizona, is a splendid example of the Queen Anne style. It is just one of several Queen Annes found in Prescott.

and varied Queen Anne designs rise behind wrought-iron fences and stately old trees. Another grouping of Queen Annes stands along Union Street, on what is often referred to as Nob Hill. Many of these large homes were constructed during the 1890s, indicating Prescott's immunity to the prevailing economic downturn that severely affected other parts of the West. Several Colonial Revival and Neoclassical structures can be seen as well. A walking tour of historic Prescott is available from the Chamber of Commerce.

BISBEE

Another center of mining activity in Arizona grew in the Mule Mountains near the Mexico border. The area was first prospected in 1875 by a man named Hugh Jones, who was looking for silver but found copper instead. Discouraged, he left empty-handed but was followed two years later by others who recognized the worth of this ordinary metal. By 1880 a small town was in place, and after outside money was invested in the claims, a flurry of copper mining activity was underway. It was not until 1892, though, that

things really got rolling, for that is when the copper giant Phelps Dodge Company built a railroad into Bisbee. With this supply line, the town could begin its expansion in earnest. By 1900 Bisbee was a bustling city of twenty thousand and one of the state's largest and liveliest metropolises.

Because of Bisbee's relatively late start, most of its structures were constructed after the turn of the century. Consequently, the town is mostly post-Victorian in design. Nevertheless, it offers a vivid glimpse into the past with its lavish and varied architecture. In 1902 the Copper Queen Hotel was erected at the center of town, across from the 1895 Phelps Dodge General Office Building. Brewery Gulch, just around the corner, was the site of Bisbee's infamous days of free-for-all fun, and the Pythian Castle, constructed in 1904, is perched on a hillside east of the gulch. Sporting Bisbee's only clock tower, this highly visible edifice originally served as the Knights of Pythias Lodge. A walking tour of Bisbee's steep and narrow streets is available from the Chamber of Commerce.

89

Idaho

As Colorado's "Fifty-niners" gold rush continued on into the 1860s, Idaho likewise became the destination of thousands of gold seekers, either as "dissatisfied refugees" from the Colorado camps, experienced miners from California and Nevada, or wide-eyed greenhorns from countless other locales. Historian Hubert Howe Bancroft wrote, "The miners of Idaho were like quicksilver. A mass of them dropped in any locality, broke up into individual globules, and ran off after any atom of gold in their vicinity" (Paul 1974). Despite this erratic enthusiasm, Idaho began to experience the rapid growth of new towns, as a burgeoning mining industry along with strong agricultural growth led to economic prosperity.

Idaho's isolation slowed its development. A maze of mountain ranges and numerous deep river canyons left few natural routes into this rugged wilderness. Early on, steamboat traffic utilized the Columbia and Snake rivers, making Lewiston an advance supply point in northern Idaho. To the south, the Oregon Trail passed over one of the few respites in the rugged landscape, the Snake River Plains. Few other suitable access routes existed.

Resourcefulness, rather, was the key to growth in Idaho. Farming communities made use of Idaho's rich grasslands and fertile soil, and as mining came to the Boise Basin, pack trails and toll roads were developed to serve the expanding camps and towns. The Transcontinental Railroad allowed easier overland freighting from points in Utah to Boise, but it was not until the long-awaited arrival of the Oregon Short Line and the Northern Pacific Railroad in the 1880s that Idaho's transportation problems were eased. As was the pattern in most Rocky Mountain towns, Victorian architecture developed more rapidly after the arrival of the railroad.

This opulent home in Boise, Idaho, is typical of the city's many fine Victorian residences.

BOISE

When a party of prospectors found gold in the hills of southwestern Idaho in 1862, an inevitable sprinkling of mining camps materialized by year's end in the area known as the Boise Basin. Within a year, Fort Boise was established in the valley below to offer protection from Indian raids for the new settlers. Simultaneously, a townsite was laid out between the Boise River and the fort, a sawmill was soon built, and Boise, a town of deliberate design, began to form. Many travelers along the Oregon Trail abandoned their journey at Boise when they recognized the potential for supplying the nearby mining towns with much-needed agricultural products.

An initial concern in Boise was fire, and the town fathers sought to have as many fireproof buildings as possible by mandating brick or stone construction. Various options existed, as abundant native sandstone and adobe bricks made from river materials were both widely used. Soon, the construction of a local brick foundry further aided the city's efforts.

Well established as a supply and commercial center, Boise enjoyed a stable economy even after the decline of nearby mining towns. In 1864 Boise was selected as the state capital, an act that brought further stability to the town. As a result, the city saw considerable growth well into this century.

Boise has always been considered a cosmopolitan town, and its architecture clearly shows this trait. The first homes to utilize the Victorian theme were built during the 1870s along Grove Street. Reflecting the whims of the day, these included both Gothic Revival and Second Empire designs. Since these were some of Boise's first permanent structures, however, many were subsequently torn down to make way for an expanding commercial district. During the 1880s and '90s Boise saw dramatic growth, especially after a railroad made easy access to the area possible. The Warm Springs neighborhood, an area of town that still employs geothermal energy as a heating source, was one residential district that benefited, as were the areas around the capitol (now the State Street Historic District) and Harrison Avenue. Each of these neighborhoods contains pretentious Queen Anne, Victorian Eclectic, and post-Victorian homes and mansions.

Downtown Boise, although having had to work through the quirks of urban renewal, has several superb examples of commercial building styles, many of which are scheduled for, or have already undergone, restoration.

Among them is the Idanha Hotel, a magnificent Chateauesque structure that seems to hold court over a busy business section of Boise. Although no walking tours of Boise are in print, two books *(Historic Boise* and *The Boiseans: At Home)* by local historian Arthur A. Hart do offer detailed and fascinating exposés on the city's important homes and edifices.

MOSCOW

Moscow has the distinction of being built upon the riches of an agricultural bonanza, in contrast to those built on the wealth of the mining boom. The first settlers in the area gazed upon a valley of waist-high grass and rich black soil, named the area Paradise, and in 1871 established the first permanent settlement. With the business district and post office in full operation by 1876, the U.S. Postal Service requested a name change. As Moscow, the town continued to grow and thrive with early industries of flour milling, brewing, logging, and crop and livestock agriculture. The first railroad arrived in 1885, bringing its commercial benefits to the community. The creation of the University of Idaho in 1889 likewise gave Moscow another productive element.

The Latah County Historical Society on the corner of Second and Adams

The 1886 McConnell Mansion, included in the Fort Russell Historic District of Moscow, Idaho, reflects a late-Gothic influence. Today, the structure is owned by the Latah County Historical Society and is open for tours.

streets is the starting point of a walking tour of the Fort Russell Historic District. The historical society is operated out of a fascinating Gothic house built in 1886 by Idaho's first two-term governor, William J. McConnell. All of the homes on the tour were built after 1885, when the arrival of the railroad increased the availability of materials, and most are Queen Anne or Eclectic in character. These homes were built on large estates, which were later sectioned off into smaller land parcels.

Hence, post-Victorian architecture is interspersed with the older homes. It provides a good example of the evolution of the neighborhood.

LEWISTON

It is surprising to think of steamboats as part of the early history of a Rocky Mountain town, but in Lewiston the steamboat was the conveyor of goods and the key to the town's establishment as a supply center for the gold fields of Idaho. Pacific Coast merchants were aware of the competition they faced from suppliers in Salt Lake City, who sent goods to Idaho across overland routes. In response, they sent their goods in by way of the Columbia and Snake rivers to Lewiston, where pack mules then penetrated the mountains to supply the gold camps beyond.

High on the bluffs overlooking the Snake River at its confluence with the Clearwater are the resplendent homes of Lewiston's successful pioneers. Known as Normal Hill, this neighborhood had to wait until water service reached it in 1892. Hence many homes are post-Victorian, but are worth looking at just the same. The commercial district down along the river has some early commercial architecture and is featured in the Thomas W. Campbell walking tour.

OAKLEY

Oakley is a town that failed to observe the proprieties of most rural farm communities and instead embellished its streets with Victorian homes and stately commercial buildings. Settled by both Mormons and cattlemen in the late 1870s, these early pioneers were staunch supporters of a high standard of living despite the frontier environment of south-central Idaho. Influenced by the architecture of Salt Lake City's Victorian mansions, Oakley's residents built their houses with a similar style and finesse. With three, and possibly four, brick yards, plus a local quarry, most of Oakley's homes were constructed of brick and stone. Large families lived in these predominantly Queen Anne structures, and as children married and had families of their own, they built homes similar to those of their parents. Although a town of eight hundred, Oakley nonetheless supports an organized preservation effort, Historic Oakley, that grew out of the first home tours over eighteen years ago. Renovation efforts are ongoing by the homeowners, and an annual guided walking tour held each June serves to highlight their efforts. Currently, the tour has some thirty-five sites listed.

WALLACE

A late-bloomer among Idaho mining communities, Wallace began as a town in 1884 in one of the richest mining districts of the West. Once the various claims of the region were laid out, the town's population grew quickly and, typically, became as wild and unruly as a boomtown could get. In 1890 a fire destroyed the downtown sector, and two years later, Wallace's first labor war broke out. In 1910 a major forest fire leveled the entire east side of town, effectively erasing much of the town's nineteenth-century architecture.

Today the entire town is listed on the National Register of Historic Places and it is currently undergoing a slow process of renovation. Presenting many examples of transitional styles from the turn of the century, Wallace also features some examples of Queen Anne and Stick styles. The pride and joy of Wallace, however, is the Northern Pacific Depot, built in 1901. In 1986 the massive structure was moved two hundred feet to make room for a highway expansion project. Today the depot is the home of the Wallace Chamber of Commerce. A walking tour encompasses the town, including commercial sites, residential buildings, and local churches.

Montana

Almost sixty years after the explorations of Lewis and Clark, rich placer mines drew a new breed of adventurer to the Montana frontier. With water access provided by the Missouri River, this section of the Rockies had received plenty of attention throughout the first half of the nineteenth century. Rival fur companies had staked out their territories along the streams and rivers, and early forts, used to establish wilderness trading posts, dotted the landscape. By 1862, however, the fur industry had been abandoned and the murmurings of "gold" produced the early boomtowns of Bannack City and Virginia City. While Montana's rich placer deposits provided the first flurry of activity, it was silver and then copper that truly propelled its mineral commerce to epic proportions. Toward the end of the nineteenth century, Montana's copper empires of Butte and Anaconda became major industrial centers of the West. The reigns of these monolithic corporate giants would prevail well into the twentieth century.

Montana encompasses a vast amount of land, much of it broad stretches of grassland. Upon this resource the cattle and sheep industry evolved into another powerful economic element, not as dominant as the mineral faction, yet nevertheless influential. In conjunction with the railroad, agriculture played a definitive role in the scheme of Montana's Victorian architecture.

Urban renewal in the 1970s produced some awkward blends of old and new architecture, yet the remaining structures still offer a vivid display of nineteenth-century commercial buildings. The Atlas Building is a particularly unusual example, with its stone sculpture of the mythical Atlas supporting a column of granite on his shoulders. The 1888 structure is topped with a large urn and a salamander (symbol of fire) descending down a finial only to be warded off by two winged dragons.

Helena's past is most visible through her homes, which include some outstanding Second Empire, Italianate, and Queen Anne structures. A couple of early Gothic Revival homes can also be found. With Last Chance Gulch as the dividing line, Helena's two main neighborhoods rise on either hillside. Highlighting the east side of the gulch is the 1885 Governor's Mansion, now a museum, and the Sanders House—notable for its construction date of 1875, eight years before the arrival of the railroad. The neighborhood west of Last Chance Gulch contains many more stately residences of Helena's pioneer families, while the Lennox Addition—an 1893 subdivision near the capitol—offers a small number of large Queen Anne homes. A walking tour is available.

BUTTE

Although Butte started as an insignificant gold placer camp in 1864, it soon grew into a mining center of international prominence. With the silver boom of the 1870s, investors began to pour huge amounts of capital into the town's various operations. Even before the railroad arrived, mining persisted as high-grade ore was shipped through Fort Benton and Corrine, Utah, while that of lower grade was stockpiled until transportation was improved or a local smelter made it economical to mill. Experienced silver miners, many veterans of the Comstock Lode in Nevada, brought much-coveted skills to Butte. By 1876 Butte was heralded as the "quartz Eldorado of the great Northwest," yet the boom did not end here. Copper brought a second economic wind, especially with a burgeoning national market maintained by the electric light and telephone. As the silver mines plunged deeper into the hillsides, copper became the most abundant element to be found. Copper soon dominated the state's economy, gaining a powerful grip on Montana's political affairs as well.

Today, the architecture of Butte offers concise testimony to the town's affluent foundation, and yet the subsequent decline of the mining industry has accounted somewhat for the preservation of the buildings. Without the economic impetus to sustain twentieth-century growth, Butte is somewhat of a municipal museum of Victorian designs and tastes. Impressive examples of the Italianate, Second Empire, and Queen Anne styles are plentiful, as are those of post-Victorian tastes. One important structure, the 1888 Copper King Mansion, is now open for tours. Butte's downtown sector reflects the severity of the city's economic slump, as most of its edifices are in need of restoration. Nevertheless, Butte, with its grand display of nineteenth-century architecture, has earned status as a National Historic Landmark.

BOZEMAN

The Gallatin Valley in the heart of the northern Rockies was the site of some of Montana's earliest farms. Taking advantage of the fertile soil and the availability of water, farmers began supplying the surrounding gold camps in the mid-1860s. By 1867 Bozeman was the principal town of the valley and boasted that it had a more secure future than the tenuous gold towns. Established by John Bozeman, the town was located on the Bozeman Trail.

With the establishment of Yellowstone National Park in 1872, the first tourist trade commenced, and the presence of an army station, Fort Ellis, contributed to a solid social climate as many West Point officers called Bozeman home. The railroad arrived in 1883, expanding the agricultural market and utilizing nearby coal deposits. In 1893 the state legislature voted to establish a state agricultural college in Bozeman, now Montana State University.

Today, Bozeman's Main Street mirrors the city's dynamic past with the various architectural elements expressed in its commercial buildings. A self-guided historical tour, produced through the efforts of the Bozeman Historic Resource Survey, details Main Street as well as the residential sections that spread out to the north and south. Of special note is the South Willson Historic District, a neighborhood that dates from 1880 to 1910. Lining this avenue, as well as those that surround it, are a number of Second Empire, Queen Anne, Neoclassical, and other twentieth-century revival styles.

LIVINGSTON

A product of the railroad's role in the settlement of the West, Livingston was established as a Northern Pacific depot in 1882, providing a commercial center

Wyoming

It is easy to think of a railroad town, but Wyoming could conceivably be called a railroad state. As the Transcontinental Railroad began to take shape and receive support from the nation, several routes were proposed and each one was vigorously promoted by its respective backer. No less than five routes were surveyed, but the Omaha to San Francisco corridor eventually won out. Despite repeated claims that it would pass through a "barren and sterile country," the rail line crossed the breadth of what is now Wyoming. Although not a big winner in the mining boom of the Rocky Mountains, Wyoming was a definite success with respect to the railroad.

Building upon the access that the railroad provided, the cattle industry soon formed a powerful lobby within Wyoming. Even Montana cattlemen joined the Wyoming Stock Growers Association so that they could utilize Wyoming rail points for shipping their livestock to market. The days of the cattle barons were glorious ones until the winter of 1886–87 when bitter cold and snow devastated the vast herds that the corporate outfits had put together.

With only minor exceptions, the majority of Wyoming's Victorian architecture is found in the towns that prospered along the Union Pacific corridor. Victorian-style homes, especially Queen Anne, continued to be built in Wyoming even after the turn of the century. One state historian attributes this to the traditional conservativism of Wyoming's residents.

The Tivoli Building in downtown Cheyenne, Wyoming, is a unique example of the Queen Anne style. Built in 1892 as a tea room, the structure was a speakeasy during prohibition. Today it houses a Chamber of Commerce Visitor Center.

CHEYENNE

The symbiosis between the Transcontinental Railroad and Cheyenne started with the official platting of the town by the railroad crew in 1867 and has never ceased; even today Cheyenne remains an important rail hub. Those initial town lots sold for one hundred fifty dollars and were quickly purchased by intrepid souls willing to stake their future in a railroad community. By winter, the track crews entered town, bringing the disassembled buildings of their last camp with them. This traveling collection of shacks earned the phrase "Hell on Wheels," reflecting the rowdy character of the city. Cheyenne narrowly escaped obsolescence when executives of the Union Pacific considered awarding Laramie the coveted role of division point for the future connecting line with Denver. Fortunately, for Cheyenne, this thought was not carried out and her fate as a major rail town was assured.

The 1870s and '80s were the years of the cattle baron, with eastern and European capital financing bovine empires. The proper residence for a prosperous rancher became an elaborate home adorning the residential section already populated by wealthy businessmen, politicians, lawyers, and doctors. As the capital of the Wyoming ter-

103

by I

l

root

cent

Hist

now

som

to tl

cont

offic

with

front

Cent

mult

denti

24th

home

and (

S A N

Heral

Coun

as it (

exam

in Ut

of Epl

and S

small

by Mc

Scand

Scand

Valley

where

and Sv

cultur

a landmark, the demolition permit will automatically go into effect after ninety days. It is hoped that within this grace period a more sympathetic buyer, or perhaps public pressure, will save the structure. If the building is within a landmark district, the commission's decision is final and a demolition permit will not be granted.

If one conclusion can be drawn from the multitude of federal, state, and local preservation laws, it is that the public's interest in preserving the nation's heritage is very strong. Other evidence of this, though, can be found in the number of citizen's organizations that have been established. Interestingly, many of these organizations work closely with or are a part of state historical agencies. The Montana Historical Society, for example, boasts of being the oldest in the West. Incorporated in 1865, it was originally a private entity but in 1891 became a state agency. The Idaho State Historical Society followed a similar path a few years later. Typically, historical societies solicit members, provide educational services, publish books and other interpretive materials, operate museums, and preserve specific historic sites and buildings.

In addition to these quasi-public organizations, many truly grassroots interest groups also exist and have been quite successful in promoting preservation causes. One such organization is the Utah Heritage Foundation, established in 1966. Besides stirring up public interest through various educational means, the Heritage Foundation has also managed to influence public policy through lobbying efforts and with a monthly newsletter that is outspoken on issues affecting historic preservation.

Additionally, the Utah Heritage Foundation has established a revolving-fund campaign to save and restore the Marmalade District of Salt Lake's Capitol Hill area. As with most revolving funds, two courses of action can be taken. One is to provide with favorable terms, loans to homeowners interested in renovating their homes, and the other involves the purchase of historic homes that come on the market. Following this, the foundation determines what restoration work will be needed and then sells the property to a buyer interested in renovating the building. Terms of sale guarantee not only the structure's existence but its restoration in a timely manner as well. After the property is sold, the money is applied toward another historic building. By concentrating its efforts in one area, the Utah Heritage Foundation is effectively preserving an entire neighborhood for future generations. At the center of the Marmalade District is the Utah Heritage Foundation's headquarters, a resplendent 1884 Gothic Revival house, which was moved from its original downtown location to make way for a new hotel.

Another important nonprofit preservation group is Historic Denver, Inc. With two thousand five hundred members, it is often touted as the largest in the nation. As with the Utah Heritage Foundation, Historic Denver is active in creating public awareness via educational resources, a monthly newsletter, and regularly scheduled tours. It also acts as a community advocate. Through acquiring easements, providing public testimony in defense of preservation causes, and maintaining contacts with the city government, Historic Denver has chalked up many successes. The first of these came in 1970 with the Molly Brown House. When this famous Denver site came up for sale, Historic Denver, Inc., was founded to purchase and then renovate it. Today the Molly Brown home is open for tours. Some of the group's subsequent victories include the Paramount Theatre, the Ninth Street Historic District, and the city's Lower Downtown.

While statewide preservation scenarios, and those of large metropolitan areas, present a staggering array of dilemmas, the protection of historical buildings in smaller Rocky Mountain communities can likewise be overwhelming. Forty-five miles west of Denver is the 1860s mining center of Georgetown. Rich in nineteenth-century structures, Georgetown is an important repository of Victorian architecture. Working diligently to preserve it since 1970 has been the Georgetown Historical Society.

Housed on the grounds of the Hamill House, the Georgetown Historical Society fulfills many of the interpretive functions of conventional historical societies, but beyond that, it has also served as the impetus of preservation practices that concern the town. It acts as an information source to property owners concerned with preserving historic buildings, and offers assistance in understanding tax laws pertaining to historic structures. It conducted a comprehensive architectural survey, and is currently working in conjunction with various government entities to conserve the town's mountain environment. In small cities like Georgetown, saving the face of the surrounding landscape is an important task, for it preserves the context within which the past unfolded. Typical of small-town preservation groups, however, the Georgetown Historical Society is plagued by

123

EPILOGUE

Sculptured detail on the Elks Lodge in Ouray, Colorado.

The presence of Victorian architecture in the Rocky Mountain West is the end result of many forces that shaped the region's development. The economic boom, produced by the mining, timber, and cattle industries; the epic arrival of the railroad to this remote land; the reigning architectural tastes of the day; and the desire of these early westerners to embellish their lives all contributed to the manifestation of Victorian building designs in the Rockies.

On a similar note, the very existence of differing stylistic themes in Victorian architecture serves to fortify the heterogeneous nature of this building genre. These styles speak of the interests and concerns of those people we call Victorians. They create a chronological overlay with which to study the era, and they offer an aesthetic mosaic that is both memorable and appealing.

But once the historical notations are made, and after the particulars of each Victorian building style are listed, two important realizations come to mind. First, the most pleasurable aspects of Victorian architecture in the Rocky Mountains come not from an inventory of facts, dates, and figures, but rather from aesthetics. To stroll a shady avenue lined with a splendid blend of Gothic Revival, Italianate, and Second Empire homes; to experience the vivacious personality of a block of bracketed storefronts; to witness the solidity of an imposing Romanesque commercial structure; or to discover an unheralded and yet brilliantly con-

We would like to thank the following people for helping to make the logistics of our travels easier: Steve Bly with the Boise Convention and Visitors Bureau, Ray Stattner of the Idanha Hotel, Linda Carlson and Joe Rutherford with The Utah Travel Council, and Jerry and Carole Sanders, owners of the Homestead Resort.

Our sincerest gratitude goes to both family and friends for their support and encouragement. To Grant Kalivoda, owner of the Camera & Darkroom in Santa Fe, thank you for the technical assistance. To our close friend Melvyn Matis, we are especially grateful for your generous support in both the field and office. And to our parents, thank you for your unfailing belief in our abilities.

Perhaps our final note of acknowledgment should go out to the many historic preservationists across the country. Without their tireless efforts, our discovery and investigation of the West's Victorian past would not have been possible. Because of their work, many generations will be able to relish this vestige of American heritage, just as we have.

INDEX